Attracting IT Graduates to Your Business

Capture the best and brightest IT talent for your company

An Coppens

Impackt Publishing
We Mean Business

Attracting IT Graduates to Your Business

First published: February 2014

Production Reference: 1050214

Published by Impackt Publishing Ltd.
Livery Place
35 Livery Street
Birmingham B3 2PB, UK.

ISBN 978-1-78300-008-1

www.Impacktpub.com

Cover Image by Jarek Blaminsky (milak6@wp.pl)

Credits

Author

An Coppens

Reviewers

Chris Bresnahan

Sarah Mottram

Commissioning Editor

Nick Falkowski

Copy Editors

Jalasha D'costa

Maria Gould

Paul Hindle

Project Coordinator

Priyanka Goel

Proofreaders

Maria Gould

Paul Hindle

Simran Bhogal

Indexer

Hemangini Bari

Production Coordinator

Melwyn D'sa

Cover Work

Melwyn D'sa

About the Author

An Coppens is the Chief Game Changer at Gamification Nation Ltd., where the vision is to make business and learning more fun and engaging. She is an award winning business coach, learning and development professional, author, and speaker.

With Gamification Nation, An offers consulting services and online learning programs to assist organizations with creating lasting experiences customers remember, by applying game psychology and game design techniques to non-game situations. She was recently ranked in the top 100 gamification consultants and innovators of 2013 with her Twitter alter ego *@GamificationNat*.

She is the author of *Leading the boss in the mirror*, a book that teaches people smart and practical ways to reduce their stress levels. This book was written with stressed executives and individuals in mind. In the book, she shares 15 years of client work and personal experience on how to deal with stress and reintroduce moments of calm back into your schedule.

She was a guest expert contributor on the RTE (Irish television) show *How Long Will You Live?* since its pilot series and continued to contribute throughout all the following series. Her clients nominated her for the European Coaching Achievement Award and proved to the European Coaching Institute that they had achieved lasting benefits from working with An as their coach.

She speaks and trains on the topics of gamification for entrepreneurs and learning, work-life balance, and leadership with passion and inspiration at conferences and in corporate settings. The feedback given at these events ranges from inspirational to making a tangible difference. She has worked with 100s of business owners, high achievers, and corporate employees to achieve a new level of skill in business development, mindset, leadership, and more.

She originally started B/Right Business Coaching in Cork, Ireland, to bring about a big business change knowledge to the small business sector, because prior to this venture An had worked with Xigma Management Consultants, Philips Electronics and Arthur Andersen Business Consulting, where she had learned big business strategies for both project management and change management. She holds a BA (Hon) in International Marketing and languages from Dublin City University and an MBA from the Open University Business School in the UK.

An is a prolific reader and will seek out further development with mentors and thought leaders worldwide to enhance her skills and improve her services for clients. She holds business and life coaching qualifications from the UK, the U.S.A., Australia, and Ireland, and is qualified as master practitioner of neuro-linguistic programming. She is currently studying toward a diploma in game design and has recently added gamification designer to her qualifications.

She became the go-to person for business startups, business growth, and work-life balance and worked extensively with clients from the Cork city and county enterprise boards as well as Enterprise Ireland.

In 2010, An took on the new challenge of becoming an internal training consultant for the media industry with a position in Modern Times Group, a broadcasting group headquartered in Stockholm, Sweden, with the largest geographical footprint in commercial radio, television, and online TV. She quickly proved her capabilities by winning the Rookie Award in Modern Services with her Strengths Based Leadership training.

Contact *An Coppens*

www.ancoppens.com

www.gamificationnation.com

E-mail: an.coppens@gamificationnation.com

Contents

> Preface

Attracting top IT talent is a challenge, especially when big names in the IT world such as Google, Facebook, IBM, and EMC are snapping up the best candidates, either through innovative recruitment techniques or by pure reputation. In this book, we will guide you through ways in which you can implement their techniques in order to gain equal traction on your recruitment efforts.

Let's start by looking at what the industry's powerhouses are doing to attract the best recruits to come and work for them.

Google

Google ranked first—for the fourth time in a row—in the 2013 Fortune Top 100 Best Companies to Work For. Not only does the organization have a great reputation, but also their office spaces have featured in numerous magazines. Google's corporate lifestyle complements the organization and is made available to its staff. In fact, during their recruitment process, Google puts together a committee made up of existing employees, who check out the new potential hires on Google Hangout. What better way to be interviewed for a job with Google than by having a bunch of Googlers taking you through a series of interviews and testing your technical skills as well as checking how you think through a problem?

Google has a clear idea of the type of person that will thrive in their environment, so they will specifically look for them. When you first apply for a position, the recruitment team will contact you in order to provide you with more information on the role. Then, the person who works in a similar role will take you through a screening to find out more about you and what your expectations are in relation to the role and the organization. These initial steps are often carried out over the phone. Once you're invited to attend an interview at a Google office, expect to have five interviews in a day with some practical tasks related to your area of specialization. The main purpose of these interviews is to find out what you're passionate about in relation to technology and to determine your problem solving ability. When the group of interviewers recommends that you should be hired, feedback is given relatively quickly. However, you should expect anywhere between four and nine interviews; this is a reduction down from 12 to 14 interviews in some cases, or even as many as 29 interviews before getting hired. Before offering you the post, a number of decision making committees jump into action.

For Reference

Here are three links that illustrate Google's hiring process:

```
http://www.google.co.uk/about/jobs/lifeatgoogle/
hiringprocess/
```
```
http://www.google.co.uk/about/jobs/lifeatgoogle/
```
```
http://www.businessinsider.com/infographics-process-of-
getting-hired-at-google-2011-10
```

What attracts IT graduates to Google is its reputation for being a people-centered organization, where passion for innovation is blended with development opportunities, career growth, top-end design workspaces created to encourage creativity and collaboration, and its widely renowned benefits, from onsite massage to games rooms, sports arenas, onsite crèche facilities, and the list goes on.

Tip

Aim to be in the Best Companies to Work For shortlist in your community.

Facebook

Another great company to work for is Facebook. Even though the company didn't make it into the Fortune 100 Best Companies to Work For in 2013, it maintains its meritocratic approach to hiring, which you may have seen in the movie "The Social Network" or in the book with the same title. The first technical employees earned their position by winning a coding competition, also known in the industry as a hack-a-thon or hack-fest. The competition element has remained within the recruitment process, and the starting point of the process is very similar to that of Google; an initial telephone screening interview with a recruiter, then with someone more role-specific. Once candidates are invited to the headquarters, they are required to take coding tests that include the more challenging end of coding languages. Hack-fests still take place and Facebook will now award winners with at least a telephone interview.

Common traits of the Fortune 100 Best Companies to Work For

If we look at the top 10 of the Fortune 100 Best Companies to Work For, we will find names of companies that may not be well known for their hiring practices or innovative benefits, but are worth checking out all the same because of their behavioral style interviewing techniques, which still work and set them apart as great companies to work for. Number two on the Fortune 100 Best Companies to Work For is SAS, number six is Netapp, and number nine is Ultimate Software.

While no original-style recruitment processes drive the other top 10 contenders, what they do have in common is a people-centered approach to structuring the organization. They have well-being and development of staff as core mottos. Original staff benefits range from onsite gyms, indoor basketball courts, ice cream trucks, and organic farms, to various perks such as health care and free holidays. But the glue that holds the companies together seems to be a solid value-driven approach to business and people. They not only want to hire the best, but also want to retain the best, and they actively work at creating a positive workplace culture.

Another organization worth highlighting is `Salesforce.com` because of their innovative use of social media to attract IT graduates. `Salesforce.com` posts jobs and job-search-related information under the Twitter hashtag *#dreamjob*, which they completely dominate even though it isn't a proprietary term. The company exploits all kinds of social networks such as their YouTube channel, where you can see several clips of staff testimonials; you can go back to their dream force conference and review various client case studies and create an online appreciation for the company, its senior managers, and their clients.

Your organization's online presence will make a difference to the way candidates perceive your company, and the old template static website is definitely a thing of the past, when job advertisements featured in newspapers and "snail" mail were the only application processes. Nowadays, you see career pages on most company websites, with the inclusion of various video clips featuring employees and their career paths, company culture, and value statements. Often, the career page is the entry point for a candidate application through an automated database system.

Tip

Have an attractive presence within the career pages on your website.

Today's candidates are web-savvy and their searches will go further than your own career pages. Social media is a vast resource and will often tell the other side of the corporate story. Being in a high position on best workplace lists is a great endorsement, because it immediately gives further validation to your employer's brand as well as providing listings on external websites, which in turn increases your Google ranking, and researching hires will find this information at the click of a button.

Social media in recruitment is definitely here to stay. While a few years ago job boards such as Monster were all the rage, their domination of that market is being eroded by the professional networking sites such as LinkedIn and the Facebook collaboration **BeKnown**. However, LinkedIn is definitely the place to be for professional connections and knowledge-sharing on companies and products, as well as research on candidates through their profiles, recommendations, and network of connections. A few organizations utilize the power of LinkedIn groups and company pages fully, and often recruiters will not systematically research potential new hires in this environment.

Tip

Top tip: Become present on social media with engaging content.

With current unemployment rates at a high and governments offering incentives to take on apprentices, the IT industry has also started to actively seek out potential trainees. Some companies, such as EMC for example, give candidates the opportunity to explore various teams through a number of projects with backing of additional training, so the apprentice or trainee will come out with a new range of skills, and in quite a few situations, a potential job offer.

At a recent learning and development exhibition, I spoke to the founders of Inspiring Interns, who said that their demand for IT interns was higher than their supply. What they saw happening in the marketplace was that banks and other financial institutions could offer higher starting salaries, which is what's attracting a good percentage of the top talent pool of IT graduates.

When you look at the organizations that attract top IT talent, they not only offer a reasonable salary, but they also offer a great package, which includes benefits, culture, and a place that people want to belong to and where they can learn throughout their career. For the purpose of this book, we will zone into "how to" questions so your organization can also excel at some of the techniques used by those that are already successful at attracting graduates in their droves.

But before we launch into how you can replicate these techniques, let's examine what it is that current IT graduates, and in particular the Millennials, also known as Generation Y (born between 1977 and 1997), want from their future employers.

What this book covers

Chapter 1, What Do IT Graduates Want?, gives an insight into some of the key behaviors and deciders of the generation of graduates that are currently joining the workforce in high numbers globally. In this chapter, you will learn:

> What are the key deciders for the generation of graduates that are currently joining the workforce? What motivates them to join a company?

> Tips on how to adapt your internal practices to include this generation of workers.

> How the communication styles differ across generations and how you can harness these to attract the new generation of IT graduates.

> What turns graduates off.

Chapter 2, Be Clear on What Your Organization Has to Offer, shows you how to put your best foot forward in promoting an organization to IT graduates, by creating unique selling points, describing the elements of the package you are presenting to the candidate, and creating the ultimate role description.

Chapter 3, Creativity Rules in Gaining Graduate Interest, shows you how to put your best foot forward in promoting an organization to IT graduates.

Chapter 4, Getting to "You're Hired", takes you from the application all the way through to the first few days on the job for your new recruit. The key topics you will learn in this chapter are as follows:

> ➤ The importance of timing as part of the recruitment process
> ➤ Narrowing down your shortlist
> ➤ Competency-based interviews
> ➤ Skills testing
> ➤ Final steps of making an offer
> ➤ Welcoming your candidate

Who this book is for

This book is aimed at hiring managers and recruiters in smaller businesses, which may not have a full HR team or would like to explore creative techniques to recruit the right IT graduates to their business.

Conventions

In this book, you will find a number of styles of text that distinguish between different kinds of information. Here are some examples of these styles, and an explanation of their meaning.

New terms and **important words** are shown in bold.

Make a Note
Warnings or important notes appear in a box like this.

Tip
Tips and tricks appear like this.

Reader feedback

Feedback from our readers is always welcome. Let us know what you think about this book—what you liked or may have disliked. Reader feedback is important for us to develop titles that you really get the most out of.

To send us general feedback, simply send an e-mail to contact@impacktpub.com, and mention the book title via the subject of your message.

If there is a book that you need and would like to see us publish, please send us a note via the **Submit Idea** form on `https://www.impacktpub.com/#!/bookidea`.

Piracy

Piracy of copyright material on the Internet is an ongoing problem across all media. At Impackt, we take the protection of our copyright and licenses very seriously. If you come across any illegal copies of our works, in any form, on the Internet, please provide us with the location address or website name immediately so that we can pursue a remedy.

Please contact us at `copyright@impacktpub.com` with a link to the suspected pirated material.

We appreciate your help in protecting our authors, and our ability to bring you valuable content.

> 1

What Do IT Graduates Want?

Millennials are entering the workforce in their thousands. This is the generation of students that have seen their parents or relatives being made redundant, that have experienced the great recession through their immediate family and friends, and as a result, they have started to shape their values and behaviors based on our current society. They have also experienced wars and other wrongs being reported through social media such as Twitter, and they understand that life will change regularly, whether you are well prepared or not.

Who are the Millennials?

The Millennials are often also named the Google or Net generation because of their comfort with all things technological. They grew up using technology and they expect employers to provide them with the same tools used in their personal life to collaborate, create, brainstorm, and network. They are hyper-connected through all types of media—physically and socially. News is sourced online and then shared across a wide range of social media networks. They love to learn and they know that there will always be new things to learn because of our dependency on technology. When they learn, they want the content to be engaging and inspiring, with an element of fun thrown in for good measure.

In his book *Grown Up Digital: How the Net Generation is Changing Your World*, Don Tapscott established a summary of the norms and characteristics critical to understanding the needs of this generation.

The Millennials can be defined as follows:

➤ Want freedom in everything they do, from freedom of choice to freedom of expression

➤ Love to customize and personalize their experiences

➤ Are the "new" scrutinizers; they make up their mind swiftly and expect their opinions to count

➤ Look for corporate integrity and openness when deciding what to buy and where to work

➤ Want to find entertainment in their work, education, and social lives

➤ Are focused on collaboration and relationship building

➤ Have a need for speed—and not just in video games

➤ Are innovators and are constantly looking for different ways to collaborate, entertain themselves, learn, and work

As an employer, accommodating or even just being cognizant of these traits is often a challenge. For a lot of organizations, it will mean that they need to rethink how work needs to be carried out, how teams work together, and how much is shared for the purpose of creativity and innovation.

In your organization:

➤ Can employees access the Internet?

➤ Can employees access social media?

➤ Can employees interact through online collaboration tools?

Millennials believe this as essential for their productivity. If you don't make the tools available, you would need a good reason for why it isn't for their use during working hours.

If I think about some of the employment terms and conditions I have seen in organizations, there may well be a cry for a massive overhaul in the coming years in order to retain the best talent. I know companies that block Facebook and chat functions or even disable the whole Internet on workstations in order to keep workers focused on the job at hand, not to mention the very restrictive clauses often found in codes of conduct or employment contracts. Obviously, at some point in time these served a purpose or were added to avoid a particular situation, but they may now be the exact reason why the new generation of workers may turn down an otherwise good offer.

When it comes to the use of social media, I have seen clauses in contracts that prohibit its use, and employers have even looked for login details for employees' personal accounts on social media, which thankfully is now deemed unethical. With blogging and microblogging through Twitter as a favorite pastime for many graduates, once again companies are trying to control what is said and not said about the inside world of work. When openness and transparency prevails, very protective and restrictive clauses may cause the Millennials to refuse offers or move on when they sense their freedom of expression is completely controlled.

Tip

Top tip: Ensure your contracts of employment, code of conduct, and internal policies also appeal to the needs of Millennials.

Millennials at work

The Chartered Management Institute in the United Kingdom commissioned a global survey entitled "Generation Y: Unlocking the talent of young managers". Through their research, Generation Y emerges as ambitious, demanding and hyper-connected, and firm believers of the thought that they can change the world. Specifically, this generation wants to:

➤ Work for an organization that does something they believe in

➤ Be self-disciplined when it comes to their learning and personal development, with 68 percent saying they want to initiate most of their own learning and development

➤ Work for organizations that are supportive, empowering, and inspiring

➤ Blend their home-life and their work-life in a fashion that allows them to work when, how, and where they want

➤ Develop new skills and good career prospects with their employer

This group of new workers is in a hurry for success. They have been using mobile phones, laptops, tablet devices, Facebook, Twitter, YouTube, and LinkedIn since their teens. Their way of finding answers is to Google search for an instant return. My own research confirms the findings of these two studies.

A PricewaterhouseCoopers (PwC) study of new college graduates found that after salary, the most important benefit in selecting a first role was training and development. When asked what kind of learning they preferred on the job, they chose as follows:

- ➤ 98 percent strong coaches and mentors
- ➤ 94 percent formal classroom-based training
- ➤ 91 percent support for further academic training
- ➤ 85 percent rotational assignments
- ➤ 62 percent e-learning

While generalizing is always a little dangerous regardless of which generation we refer to, generalizing helps to better understand future candidates, and it also helps creating an environment that they most likely want to work in, which the companies featured on the "Fortune 100 Best Companies to Work For" list have managed to achieve. Considering just one generation is slightly limiting our perspective and it doesn't necessarily give a full understanding of how similar or different we inevitably are. Presently, we have potentially three to four generations coming together in the workplace. It is important to understand all vantage points as well as differences, and you should create a strategy for the future with focus on the younger groups of workers, as they will be the driving force of any business going forward.

What is clear is that change has been with us for some time, and the speed of innovation, thanks to technology, has increased and seems to continually increase. The current generation of IT graduates grew up with diversity and very likely shared classrooms with multiple nationalities and cultures, which makes them comfortable in new cultures.

Tip

Top tip: Introduce mutual mentoring from older to younger generations and vice versa at work to help both sides understand each other's working habits and learn to accept diversity.

In a study carried out by Deloitte Consulting and the **International Association of Business Communication (IABC)**, a comparison was made regarding communication styles and preferences for each generation. In the context of understanding how the different generations may interact in the work place, it is a good idea to have a look at a summary of some of these comparisons. In most cases, those of you in charge of recruitment will potentially be from a different generation, so it is important to consider that part of attracting and understanding future generations is understanding how they communicate and how that may differ from our own preferred style, thus allowing you to tweak your career-related materials accordingly.

Here are the large categories looked at for this study. While age is a factor, preference and attitude prevails, so you can identify which category of communicators you feel most confident with. Each generation is currently represented in the work place, so it is good to compare and contrast:

- ➤ **Traditionalists:** People born before 1955
- ➤ **Baby boomers:** People born between 1956 and 1965

> ➤ **Generation X**: People born between 1966 and 1976
> ➤ **Millennials** (also known as **Generation Y**): People born between 1977 and 1997

The following table shows the communication preferences for each generation as noted by Deloitte Consulting and the International Association of Business Communicators (IABC):

	Traditionalists	**Baby boomers**	**Generation X**	**Millennials**
Style	Formal	Semiformal	Not so serious: irreverent	Eye-catching; fun
Content	Detail; prose-style writing	Chunk it down but give me everything	Get to the point—what do I need to know	If and when I need it, I will find it online
Context	Relevance to my security; historical perspective	Relevance to the bottom line and my rewards	Relevance to what matters to me	Relevance to now, today, and my role
Attitude	Accepting and trusting of authority and hierarchy	Accept the "rules" as created by the Traditionalists	Openly question authority; often branded as cynics and skeptics	OK with authority that earns their respect
Tactics	Print; conventional, mail; face-to-face dialog or by phone; some online information/ interaction	Print; conventional mail; face-to-face dialog; online tools and resources	Online; some face-to-face meetings (if really needed); games; technological interaction	Online; wired; seamlessly connected through technology
Speed	Attainable within reasonable time frame	Available; handy	Immediate; when I need it	Five minutes ago
Frequency	In digestible amounts	As needed	Whenever	Constant

With recruiters often from different generations to the IT graduates they're looking to hire, it is good to be aware of some of the current generation's key drivers as well as their communication styles.

Tip

Top tip: Write job adverts and your career information in a language and format that is appealing to current IT students

What turns Millennials off?

In preparation for this book, I did my own research of current IT graduates and asked them what would attract them to a company as well as what would turn them away from a company. Unsurprisingly, the answers I received were in line with the traits listed in the larger research samples mentioned previously.

Although I specifically didn't mention salary, it was still the number one reason to accept a role above another. The next strongest factor was the opportunity to learn and grow on a personal level as well as gain deeper technical knowledge. The third decisive factor was a tie between having a strong work/life balance and having freedom from strict rules and schedules. Work environment and benefit packages in the style of Google and Facebook were mentioned a number of times, but didn't make it into the top three. Furthermore, graduates also commented on the fact that for a lot of organizations, a strong work/life balance was often more lip service than actual reality, and they definitely wanted normal hours so that life can go on outside of work.

The answers to the question "What would turn you away from a role?" were also quite revealing and congruent with previous research. Here are some of the top reasons graduates gave for turning down a role:

- ➤ Over-restrictive tendencies
- ➤ Low level of career development
- ➤ Bad salary
- ➤ Bad product
- ➤ No flexibility and freedom on how the work is carried out
- ➤ Being squeezed for every ounce of your energy and skills; overworked
- ➤ No appreciation for work/life balance
- ➤ Uninteresting role and work

IT graduates would rather have organizations keep their promise close to reality instead of promising the moon, sun, and stars when the reality comes well short. They are eager to learn and develop, and they may consider a balanced package over a high salary with 24/7 expectations. What also came out was the expectation of graduates to have experience while, by and large, that will not be the case, and this will only end up frustrating both ends of the equation.

My personal research only accepted answers from IT graduates, whereas some of the other studies mentioned took just age as the main selection category, and yet the results were strikingly similar.

Tip

If you are currently struggling to attract IT graduates of the present generation, I would strongly encourage you to invite a group of students into your organization to give you a frank verdict of what you should improve on in order to attract them in the first place and to keep them for the longer haul.

Summary

The intention of this chapter was to give you an insight into some of the key behaviors and deciders of the generation of graduates that are currently joining the workforce in high numbers globally.

In this chapter, we have learned:

➤ What the key deciders are for the generation of graduates that are currently joining the workforce—what motivates them to join a company

➤ Tips on how to adapt your internal practices to include this generation of workers

➤ How the communication styles differ across generations and how you can harness these to attract the new generation of IT graduates

➤ What turns graduates off

I hope that by sharing these ideas, I am also making you think about your company, the benefits you offer or could potentially consider in the future, and your internal policies.

In the next chapter, you will learn how to implement the attraction policies and procedures used by some of the industry's greats.

>2

Be Clear on What Your Organization Has to Offer

With most organizations now requiring IT graduates, including established, well-known names such as those mentioned in *Chapter 1, What Do IT Graduates Want?*, the competition for talent is tough. So, in this chapter you will be provided with tips and templates that will help you identify what you can offer candidates, and you will also find help for interviewers.

Recruitment, in my opinion, is a blend of sales and marketing activity with patterns similar to that of the dating game. Therefore, throughout this book, I will draw on concepts from both the world of sales and marketing as well as dating.

Your unique selling points

The term **unique selling points** comes from the world of sales and marketing, and was originally used to showcase the unique benefits a product or service would offer above that of other competing products on the market. In this very competitive IT market, I believe it is very relevant to introduce the term "unique selling points" to your organization.

Answering the question, "What makes your organization unique?", isn't that easy. If you haven't got a prepared answer in mind, it will make your organization look bad in the minds of candidates, and it will potentially make you blend in with the majority of companies in your industry as opposed to standing out and looking attractive to a prospective candidate.

Defining your unique selling points

To assist you in deciding on your unique selling points and communicating this effectively to potential candidates, we will now share a number of ways to deduce them.

Online surveys

An excellent yet time-consuming way of coming up with a unique selling point is to ask those that know the organization best to describe the company in their own words. You can do this through a simple survey online with employees, clients, and suppliers.

Tip

Survey monkey (www.surveymonkey.com) and Google Drive document templates (requires a Gmail account to access drive.google.com) offer easy-to-create online survey templates.

The following are some suggested questions to ask in your survey:

➤ How would you describe the company in your own words?

➤ If you had to describe the company in three key words, what would they be?

➤ How would you recommend the company to potential candidates, clients, and suppliers?

The challenge with online surveys is the response rates. Typically, a 10 percent return is good, so you may need to follow-up with face-to-face or phone communications. Low cost incentives or prize draws, depending on the available budget, can also help boost survey response rates. Some marketing departments have a pre-existing research panel who are called upon for market research. These individuals are highly receptive and could also help in this situation. You should also explain the significance of this survey for your company and how the results will be used so your contacts understand how much you value their input and opinion. The best way is to keep the survey short and anonymous; that way, you ensure both completion as well as result integrity. The potential side effect of pursuing this approach is that you may find out that your organization isn't pictured as rosy as you would like it to be, in which case you are better off addressing this as a first priority, thus improving the perception of your company. Either way, once you have the results of the survey, you may choose to go with the perception of your existing audience and narrow down the answers into a few key statements. Three to five key points is a good number to aim for; if you choose too many key points, it will once again dilute your message. In my view, the survey approach is the most honest way of identifying your unique selling points.

Self-defining your unique selling points

If time isn't on your side or you are in a start-up organization, you can also decide what your unique selling points are as a management team and work toward instilling them from that point forward. If you are an existing organization where marketing teams have already decided on their unique benefits, a simple copy and paste may be sufficient, or a little adaptation to suit the recruitment purpose may well suffice. In fact, the process is similar to the online survey, with the main difference being the responding target audience. I would suggest that you do this together with the management team and recruitment decision makers. I would also suggest that you brainstorm answers to the same questions on the online survey:

> ➤ How would you describe the company in your own words?
> ➤ If you had to describe the company in three key words, what would they be?
> ➤ How would you recommend the company to potential candidates, clients, and suppliers?

Once you have a number of answers and opinions brainstormed, prioritize and narrow down the preferred options for inclusion in your recruitment information. When you decide on the key unique selling points, ensure that they are readily available to everyone in the company involved in the recruitment process and, ideally, that they are consistent in terms of information about the company. Three to five strong unique selling points are enough.

Testing your unique selling points

In marketing, it is always recommended to test and measure your messages and actions so that when you have decided on your shortlist of unique selling points, you can go on to test their validity. Testing doesn't have to be a labored process, but just a double-check to ascertain your communication is a good reflection of reality.

Your most recent hires are the best people to help you test your unique selling points with recruitment in mind. They have already chosen your company and will be in the best position to confirm quite swiftly whether those perceived points are accurate. However, there is a risk with new members of staff that they will simply agree because they will be looking to impress. In this case, allow a discussion of this topic and opinions to be shared. You can do this by having a facilitated focus group with a neutral facilitator who encourages open discussion.

You can also opt for opening testing to any number of employees, including all those in the organization. However, the best way to receive quality input is through focus groups, ideally with a neutral facilitator.

If in the definition process you opted for an online survey, you may go back to the contacts on your survey with the results and your take on it. During the process of building a lasting relationship with them, this also may well show that you truly value their opinion and may automatically create the perception of feeling part of the end result, which in my view can only be positive.

What else can you offer?

You have done the work and have come up with some compelling unique selling points, so what else is there that you should consider in your recruitment proposition? When we looked at what current IT graduates are looking for, we could clearly identify some common factors, so let's look at how you can create these for your organization, no matter what size or length of tenure you have in your industry or community.

Company culture

Every organization has a unique way of working together—this is what you would call the company culture. It includes the unspoken rules and practices, but may also define the type of graduate that would be a great fit to the team. Culture is often reflected in the dress code as well as communication interactions with potential candidates.

To make it easy for you, here are some typical counter pole descriptions of cultural values. If all you did was choose which side of the polarity you found yourself on and described this in a paragraph in your recruitment page, you have probably captured enough information for candidates to make their minds up. Once again, if you can test these statements' validity with your existing employees, you will have a stronger case. You should be as truthful as possible, because candidates will find out for themselves soon enough, and if it turns out in the first few weeks of employment inside the company that the culture was badly portrayed, you will have instantly created a lack of trust and potential loyalty, so it is better to be truthful.

Although Millennials look for similar things in a broad sense, some individuals will still thrive better in a structured, more traditional environment while others will work better in an informal, unstructured, or start-up scenario. So, the following is my list of cultural polarities (with the health warning that there obviously may be even more choices than the ones listed here):

- ➤ Formal versus informal
- ➤ Hierarchical versus no levels
- ➤ Structured versus unstructured
- ➤ Traditional versus innovative
- ➤ Client-focused versus product-focused
- ➤ Tenured versus meritocracy
- ➤ Collaborative versus autonomous
- ➤ Autocratic versus consensus
- ➤ Established versus start-up
- ➤ Fun versus serious

When graduates do their research before an interview, they will quickly find indicators of the preceding listed values. In my view, there are no right or wrong indicators in the value list—some will fit and others won't, but that is important in the selection process on both sides. As a deduction of the inner culture in your company, you can start thinking about the kind of graduate that would fit better in your team. Are you looking for someone to blend in or are you looking for someone to bring fresh ideas and stir up old ways?

Salary

Salary is often mentioned as a deciding factor for IT graduates, yet most of them come with expectations higher than their experience level indicates. Those that want remuneration above anything will always go for the highest offer. However, communicating the salary early on in the recruitment process can also eliminate a lot of time-wasting. If you include the salary in the job advert, it will clearly indicate the level of candidate you are after as well as give a value resonance to the role. If you exclude it from the role, you may receive more applications, which may increase the need for a screening phone call follow-up, unless a job application requirement is to state salary expectations.

When deciding on salary, always keep in mind what the average is for the industry and position on offer as well as what you as an organization can afford to offer. You can find salary benchmark studies on most job board websites or targeted industry websites. The following are two we found useful for the U.S. and the UK:

➤ `targetjobs.co.uk/career-sectors/it-and-technology/286195-what-graduate-salary-can-i-expect-in-an-it-job`

➤ `www.highfliers.co.uk/download/GMReport13.pdf`

When you know that the salary isn't as high as other companies in the industry due to your own business constraints, offering a valuable package becomes very important. As we know from the research in previous chapters, salary is important, but once a basic level of comfort is acquired, the other softer factors become more important. Let's look at these in a bit more depth.

Benefits

Most of the Fortune 100 Best Companies to Work For have a great list of benefits on offer, which are not always a feasible internal option for every employer. However, with a bit of creativity and negotiation, you can offer similar packages without additional financial investment on your part. The best advice I can give is to think outside the box and aim locally.

Local businesses in the current economic climate should support one another, which is why I urge you to explore, in your immediate surroundings, what is on offer. When you have identified a few local businesses to partner with, look to meet with the owners and managers to negotiate a win-win solution.

The win-win proposition for a local business is often as simple as providing extra customers by advertising their services internally to your employees—you and your employees will then get a discount and additional benefits. In most community-based locations, you will find the following businesses that may offer great partnership opportunities:

- ➤ Restaurants
- ➤ Hairdressers
- ➤ Beauty salons
- ➤ Gyms
- ➤ Local stores

When your organization is set in a rural community or an industrial park where the preceding outlets are not readily available, you may need to be even more creative and look further afield for providers who may offer an on-site or delivery service. For example, does a nearby sandwich bar offer a delivery service for which you could negotiate a discount? Is there a hairdresser, beautician, or massage therapist who could trade on-site, and would you allow your staff to use these services during office hours? Alternatively, pool resources with other companies in the business park in order to fund a restaurant or delivery service. Other key scenarios to explore are shuttle services or main pick-up points. For typical benefits such as pensions, health insurance, and employee assistance schemes, which most organizations offer these days, you can consider offering flexibility in what employees can opt in or out of.

A great benefit scheme I have come across in my career was an organization that told me at the start of my employment, based on my level of experience, how much the company would make available to me and the various choices I had available to spend that budget on. After reflecting for two weeks, I finally chose my package, and once a year I had options to allow me to review the budget and make changes. The options included newspaper subscriptions, pension, buying additional holidays, health insurance, parking, meal vouchers, and much more.

Another benefit to explore is membership cards; for example, a culture card for local cultural events at a discount or preferential rates, or an eating out card for restaurants. In most communities, these schemes are already in existence, and they are often just one phone call away from making it to the list of services that could be available for your staff. Again, this would be a win-win situation because the membership card issuer would receive a list of additional members without the need for a promotion campaign.

Charitable work (or time off for this purpose) or financial contributions for charity may also be a consideration to include in your benefits. If your organization already contributes in kind or financially, make sure this is publicized. The current generation of graduates wants to make a difference. While the graduate role may in itself not be seen as contributing to the greater good of the community, you can still appeal to this aspect for the graduate hire by giving them the opportunity to dedicate time to a cause or charity of their choice.

Once your list of benefits and options is complete, the key is to make this information readily available to existing staff so that when it hits the mark, they will be doing the selling for you. Also, in your recruitment documentation, give a description of your key benefits and especially the most popular schemes as valued by your existing employees.

Location

When it comes to careers, what plays a critical role in decision-making is property marketing and retail location. Travel and experiencing a different culture is often on the agenda of recently-graduated candidates. Play into this value by offering a description of all the great things in your immediate environment. Are you in a metropolitan hub or a rural idyll? What do the hip young people living in your neighborhood do with their free time?

If you offer a relocation package and any assistance with finding housing, you may well have an advantage over organizations closer to the graduates' original base. The positive part of offering a relocation package is the fact that you extend your potential recruitment pool. However, be aware that for some graduates, this will prove to be a step too far, and you may lose some recruits in the first few months if their transition doesn't run smoothly. The more support you can give to your internationally mobile recruits, the quicker you can gain return on your investment and the more loyalty you will create with them.

Your work environment itself is also something to give consideration to, especially in comparison with what the best in the IT world are offering. Google offices worldwide offer innovative design, colorful break areas, and rest/play zones to encourage productivity and creativity. My advice is to go and visit these offices and find out on your budget what you can emulate. Make the most of the space you have, even on a smaller scale. If you can work together with interior designers specialized in producing effective workspaces, by all means invest in it for the long term.

If your location is not desirable due to its neighbors or physical location, you actively want to minimize the negatives by creating (safe) transport and a great interior as well as focusing on the benefits of working for the company.

Opportunity and development

As you saw in the previous chapter, the new generation of workers is looking for opportunities to learn and grow, so you want to be very clear about their options in all your recruitment material. If you have an established business, the opportunity may be to learn from experienced colleagues. The key in this situation is to specify how this will be done, whether it is on the job learning side by side with experienced staff, a mentoring scheme, or formal training sessions.

If you are a start-up, the opportunity may well be to get involved in the development and future shaping of the organization as well as having the chance to gain a leadership role when the company grows. In a start-up, the responsibilities given to a graduate may be a lot wider than in an established organization.

What most graduates are looking for is an opportunity to further develop their skills and climb the career ladder. The more you can clarify how this works in your company, the better informed the candidate will be; which in turn results in a better fit. If you don't have this information readily available for a candidate to find in their research, do expect questions in relation to this at the interview stage.

When it comes to learning and development, the expectation isn't that every organization has a training department, but rather that development is seen and acted upon, so explore all the available options within your budget. Internal mentoring schemes are mainly a time investment that can create exponential results. What you can also do is invite internal experts or project leaders to speak about their work at company breakfasts, lunches, or team meetings, which again may be very appropriate and interesting. If you have a structured training program available, this can be one of your unique selling points, and if it doesn't make it to the list, make absolutely sure that it is a known item.

The following are things to consider around training:

- Do you offer internal training courses?
- Do these courses lead to certification?
- Do you have an e-learning system in place?
- Do you offer external training support for job-related courses?
- Have you got informal learning events taking place?

The thing to understand about current IT graduates is that they know learning will be key for their future, and they may see job-hopping as a way to gain quality experience. If you want to encourage them to stay longer, the key is to provide the learning opportunity inside your organization and to encourage them to do it by providing them with time for learning.

Creating a role description

Now that you have a good idea of how to explain what your organization has to offer to a potential recruit, you want to spend some time on designing a role description.

A great role description includes a list of duties the individual will need to carry out on a day-to-day basis, the skills you want the ideal candidate to have, and the personal attributes you look for in a candidate. The advice here again is to keep it as real as possible, as overselling or underselling may lead to a bad role fit and wasted recruitment time.

The starting point of a job advert is either the organization description or the role description. If the job advert starts with the role description, the organizational description and any references to packages should follow. In any case, you need both elements for a great job description.

The following are the elements essential in creating a good role description:

Description heading	Questions to answer
Purpose of the role	Why does the job exist?
	Why is the job important to the organization?
Reporting line	Who does this role report to?
	How does this role fit in the organization?
Responsibilities	What will an employee in this role will be doing?
	What are the 8 to 12 key duties this role looks after?
Skills	What are the skills you want a potential candidate to have?
	What are absolute must-have qualifications and skills?
	What are the desirable additional skills and qualifications?
	What are the top 8 to 12 skills key to performing this job well?
Personal attributes	What kind of person would work well in this role?
	What are the personal attributes you are looking for in a candidate?
	(Think soft skills, personality, and values)

When you are designing this role description, always involve the reporting manager or have them develop it. If it is a brand new position, research online what other organizations similar to yours have included in their role descriptions and align with them.

In addition to the essential items listed previously, you may want to specify salary, although this isn't essential, and in most cases, is not expected. Typically, salary is a deciding factor, and indicating it up front will also set the tone for the type of candidate that will apply, so it is entirely your choice whether to include the salary or to just look for their expectations based on their application.

Summary

This chapter showed you how to put your best foot forward when promoting an organization to IT graduates by:

> ➤ Creating unique selling points
> ➤ Describing the elements of the package you are presenting to the candidate
> ➤ Creating the ultimate role description

In the next chapter, we will explore practical and creative techniques for attracting IT graduates with examples from well-known IT organizations.

>3

Creativity Rules in Gaining Graduate Interest

In the war for great talent, creative approaches are emerging every year. Some of the best-known names in the IT industry are often the pioneers, so we will use their examples to illustrate how you can also succeed with approaches that have been tried and tested.

Use these options to work out how you can execute them on a local scale for your budget and with your existing team. It may require a bit of creativity, but we are confident that the examples and suggestions given can be equally effective for smaller companies.

Developing an attractive online presence

For the Internet-savvy generation, having an attractive online presence is important. These days, just having a website isn't enough; you need a presence on social media such as LinkedIn, Facebook, YouTube, and Twitter. When a candidate researches your organization, the first thing they will do is enter the company name into a search engine, so it is always good for you to know what comes up in that search and to ensure all your online activities push your own site to the top of the list.

In order to make this section more practical, I am going to assume that you already have a website; we will work from that starting point.

Career pages on your website

The minimum you should have on your website is a career page where you share the benefits of working for you, the unique selling points about your company, an insight into the culture of the organization, and what life is like as an employee on a day-to-day basis. Then you need to offer a searchable facility to browse open career opportunities and the application process.

These features are just the minimum, so if you want to be truly attractive, you need a lot more than the essentials. The best way to explain what you should aim for is to direct you to some great examples.

Let's look at `http://careers.microsoft.com`.

When you click on the careers home page of Microsoft, you have the option to choose whether you are a graduate or a working professional, and also your location or the location where you are looking for a position. Once you are through this filtering process, you have the following pages available (when choosing, for instance, Graduate and United Kingdom):

- ➤ Home
- ➤ Meet Microsoft
- ➤ Find Your Fit
- ➤ Apply Now
- ➤ Graduates

On the home page, you are invited to discover more about the potential roles on offer, including third-party reputable endorsements that testify why Microsoft—all over the world—is a great place to work. From the first page and in all the subsequent pages, you are invited to interact with Microsoft on social media, to ask questions on Facebook, and to follow some employee blogs.

 Tip
Invite interaction on social media or blogs.

When we delve a little bit deeper into the Graduate tab, here are the options:

- ➤ What It's Like Here
- ➤ Our Roles
- ➤ What's In It For You
- ➤ Meet Our Students
- ➤ University Events
- ➤ Application Process

On each page, you can immediately press a huge Apply Now button to start the process, and all the career pages are attractively interlinked with graphics and various click-through options. Each photograph includes a short caption that tells potential candidates why this person is a perfect fit for Microsoft; the information given is usually personal as opposed to work-related, with the key aim to build a relationship and the attractiveness factor for young people with similar hobbies.

Tip
Use attractive graphics and quotes that appeal to your audience.

Both the Our Roles and Meet Our Students pages include video clips of existing employees and graduates giving their version of life at Microsoft. Videos are a must-have because with smartphones and the ease of uploading to channels such as YouTube, no organization should have any excuses for not including videos on their website. The types of video clips to include are of people in career tracks that are attractive to your target audience of IT graduates, people talking about their jobs, life at your organization, and in each of them you obviously want a balanced yet positive approach.

Tip
Must-have: Videos on your career pages.

Your presence on social media

The main channels I will explore with you for social media are LinkedIn, Facebook, Google+, YouTube, and Twitter. The thing to remember on social media is that trends, opinions, and preferences fluctuate, so it is important to keep your content and contributions fresh and up-to-date in order to maintain interest. You may just want to choose one of the social channels and run with that, rather than spreading your presence so thin it isn't remotely doing your company justice. Follow what the greats in your industry are already doing and learn from their example.

LinkedIn

In my view, for professional purposes, every organization hiring candidates from the IT realm or other should have a presence on LinkedIn. It provides you with a ready-made and searchable job board, and it allows you to set up a company page.

The setting up process is very simple:

1. Go to `http://www.linkedin.com/companies` and click on **Add a Company**.
2. Fill in the form (note that only employees with a company e-mail may complete this).
3. Edit the page (add in all the great information about your organization).
4. Go to the Career tab and add in potential open opportunities as well as the unique selling points and cultural information about your organization. Activating this tab allows you to post jobs.

At a minimum, the passive approach for using LinkedIn will give your potential candidates the opportunity to link up with your employees and connect with you through their professional network. When you start actively posting current vacancies, you can activate your existing network of employees and have them introduce your company to potentially interesting candidates.

If you want to take your LinkedIn activity further, you can also research potential candidates by checking out their testimonials, projects, previous history, and recommendations. Simply going on their profile will allow you to do this.

The other way to create a positive profile about your company and keep people interested is to share press releases and interesting product information so that anyone that follows your organization will see this show up in their information stream. In addition, you could encourage experts in your company to contribute to groups and you could actively search for candidates in groups. Groups are formed around specific skills and interests, and IT groups on LinkedIn are among the largest groups online.

Tip

Set up a LinkedIn company page and post open vacancies on the job board.

Facebook

While LinkedIn is clearly the front-runner in professional networking, Facebook is still the largest social network. A lot of students network and participate in social sharing and gaming on Facebook before ever joining LinkedIn.

A lot of companies create a Facebook page to promote products and host online competitions. The most effective career pages on Facebook have a specific social purpose, such as for alumni or former employees. Identify what type of conversation would encourage students to engage and build a page for that purpose. For instance, Microsoft has a Women at Microsoft page.

On Facebook, your page is rated by the number of followers or number of "likes" and how many people are talking about it. In order to have people talk about your page, you need fresh content regularly and I would highly recommend that you curate comments and posts, without taking away too much of the social aspects.

Make a note

A good example of a career page with some social personality is the Dell page (`www.facebook.com/DellCareersEMEA`).

Dell posts regular updates and a combination of photos and quotes. All their jobs are posted with a link back to their careers website pages, job advice articles, and quotes.

Setting up a page requires you to have a personal profile on Facebook first, and then to the right of your newsfeed, you will find a header called Pages, which when clicked, gives you the option to create your own page. Facebook tends to change rules and regulations fairly regularly, so it is good to keep an eye on their help files, which are easy to follow. The following is the official link to setting up a Facebook page for business, which in addition gives you best practice tips on how to make the most of your page: `www.facebook.com/business/build`

Tip

A Facebook career page needs to be alive with regular fresh content.

Google+

Google is the most widely used search engine, so in order to increase your chances of being found, a Google business page is recommended with links back to your career pages. Just like Facebook, Google likes fresh content and will rank you higher on their search engines if you have regular new contributions. The suggestions given for Facebook apply to Google and nothing stops you from posting similar content to all your social media.

To set up your page, all you need to do is follow the instructions on the following page and get started: `www.google.com/+/business/`

YouTube

Once you have a Google account, you have all you need to set up a YouTube channel, and thanks to the close links of Google and YouTube, video ranks highly on the search engine list for new content. All the best companies to work for actively use video, so I highly recommend that you invest time in creating either professionally-created content or become smart-device-savvy and have fun creating clips of employees, thought-out leadership moments, company events, and so on, and launch your own channel on YouTube. To come across as authentic, make your content look "user-generated". Just like a third-party endorsement, user-generated content will come across as more credible with your target audience.

Most smartphones allow you to upload your video directly to YouTube, and then within YouTube you can edit the clips.

In order for people to go back from YouTube to your website, include the full URL of your domain name to your relevant web page, and also all the keywords potential candidates may search for in relation to your company.

Make a note

In terms of career-based channels, the following are the best we came across:

- www.youtube.com/user/ZapposFamilyCareers
- www.youtube.com/user/lifeatgoogle

Both Zappo and Google capture videos of employees in a natural and informal way while at work and involved in regular company business.

In order to create additional industry credibility, you may even take your videos a step further than just career-related, by taking a leaf out of Cisco's book; their YouTube channel is branded and contains thought leadership related content. The channel has the same look and feel as the Cisco website and the content helps build reputations, and is also interesting for technical users, potential clients, and potential new hires interested in technology. I highly recommend taking a look at their channel, www.youtube.com/Cisco.

Even if your current video creating ability isn't perfect, it is a commonly-used tool among the IT graduate population; even a well-thought-through content strategy about your core business can add credibility. The best video clips are around three minutes long and include between one to three key messages. The more natural your employees look, the higher the credibility; rehearsed and acted content will be spotted and may take away from your positive intentions.

Twitter

The best example of the use of Twitter in my view comes from Salesforce.com, who dominate the hash-tag dream job: #dreamjob.

Twitter allows you to share short updates in 140 characters or less and allows you to add links, video, and photos to these updates. In the area of recruitment, this medium is vastly underused. The objective of Twitter is to start conversation, trigger retweets, and engage in bite-size chunks of information. Unless you are able and willing to add tweets daily and encourage your employees to do the same, don't start.

When you look at the Salesforce Jobs Twitter page, twitter.com/salesforcejobs, you will not only find a combination of tweets from the recruitment team with vacancies, but you'll also find great updates of different events taking place and links to blogs or articles relevant to the company and industry. What is also very attractive is the branded background embedded with positive words, some of which are hash tags. The company advertises its own career pages in the introduction at www.salesforce.com/dreamjob. If you want to get in touch with them via Twitter, they recommend using the hash tag #dreamjob.

If you can find a word that resonates with your business and can make a link on your career pages as well as your Twitter presence, by all means go for it. In my view, this is one of the hardest channels to use effectively. Again, the key is delivering fresh content every day, and as it is limited to 140 characters per tweet, this means you need to be extremely focused. You can generate quite a following by encouraging your employees to follow you and obviously spend time creating connections too. If you have senior managers following your career account and contributing, just like the CEO of Salesforce, Marc Benioff, does—every few days he shares some top news or articles and also gives public praise for well-done results, you gain instant credibility.

 Tip
Encourage your CEO to contribute to your career Twitter page.

The short summary of all things social media for your career pages is as follows:

➤ Choose at least one social media channel to focus on and create a presence
➤ Add fresh content daily
➤ Encourage contribution and interaction
➤ Brand your social media
➤ Be creative in order to stand out from the crowd

Setting up and running a valuable apprenticeship, internship, or trainee program

Another creative way of attracting IT graduates is offering an opportunity to gain experience, which is highly valuable for the future career prospects of the candidate. In effect, inviting students into your organization is like allowing them to test drive their potential career. The biggest positive is that both you and the candidate will learn whether the fit is right for you and them.

Let's look at the differences between the following three options:

➤ **Apprenticeship**: A student joins a company and is actively trained to learn the skills required by a dedicated mentor; the focus is very much on actively learning on the job and intensive training is expected. Apprenticeships tend to be regulated in most countries, so you may need to enquire with your local authorities on how to comply with laws and regulations in relation to these contracts.

➤ **Intern**: A current student from a local university or school joins your company on a short-term internship, which may be part of their course requirement and it usually means that they give you their time in return for the experience you can offer. A salary may or may not be expected but feedback and instructions are required. Often, summer jobs can be classed as internships and some organizations have competitions at local colleges to have the best compete for a small number of coveted places. The trade-off is experience in return for time; ideally, you instruct the student to make the most of their time and gain a valuable contribution.

➤ **Trainee**: A qualified graduate applies to join a trainee program, which entails a level of on-the-job formal training and mentoring, and upon successful completion of the program, a trainee is expected to join the organization in a particular function. This is effectively a paid employee on a longer development track.

To be successful at running any of these programs, you need to give some thought as to what you are trying to achieve and what is realistic in your organization, because all three options will require dedicated time investment on your part as the employer and also varying degrees of training investment.

Getting the most out of apprenticeships

The apprentice will probably require the highest level of time and training, yet when you have a very specific way of working with specialist skills to be learned, that aren't necessarily considered in courses, it may well prove to be a good investment of time. For their first number of projects, apprentices will work with supervision and have many approval points along the way. However, on a positive note, you may have created a very loyal employee for the future, upon successful graduation of the program.

Getting the most out of internships

When it comes to internships, I have heard several stories about students being reduced to coffee runs and filing duties because no one in the organization has spare time to train them to do something worthwhile. For an internship to be meaningful and the experience to leave a positive reflection on your business, invite the students to work on a specific project, so that they can experience your real work environment, and invite them to shadow more experienced workers. This is an opportunity for your company to get fresh and new valuable feedback, and potentially trigger innovations. Both sides have the opportunity to try each other out for fit and potential employment down the line. Expect to spend a minimum of one hour or more daily with the intern for supervision and instruction, throughout the duration of their experience with your organization. If the internship forms part of an educational requirement, your feedback about the individual may determine their grades, and equally, they will be talking about your company to their peers.

Getting the most out of trainees

Finally, trainees are already qualified candidates who will have gone through some sort of selection process. This requires specific training from you, to take up the position you promised them, once they successfully complete their trainee program. This tends to be a 12 month training and practical program, where candidates prove themselves in various challenges, which range from exams to presentations and business-specific projects. In order for a program to succeed, you need to ascertain training has been well prepared and organized before recruiting candidates; use this also as part of the selling point for the program.

For each program, I suggest having a selection process whereby candidates send in an application form, a CV, and a cover letter or a competition for selection. I would definitely recommend that you meet candidates during the interview process, to find out about their motivation and real interest in the role, as well as their attitude and enthusiasm. The more merit-based the program is, the more coveted the places will be, and potentially the level of quality of the candidates will be higher.

Make a note

Best practice for all three programs

Have a selection process for a place in the program

Have a dedicated program manager

Predetermine the training track

Ensure specific projects are available to work on

Give feedback regularly

Organizing a graduate competition or hack-fest

Competition for recruitment purposes, also known as "gamification" is a relatively new concept and it is a technique that has mostly been used by the IT industry, with coder challenges, multidiscipline hack-fests, engineering contests, and actual computer or video games. One example of an extended competition, which is outside the IT industry, is the television show called "The Apprentice", which aims at finding a top-class candidate through a number of challenges to work for a successful entrepreneur. Keep it real—keep your contest strictly technical.

Choosing your problem

The premise for competition is to have a complex problem, which will attract the real problem solvers from the student community. Facebook is known to have hosted this kind of competition, albeit with an alcohol factor attached. They hired their first employees in this way and to this day they still host some competitions, which lead to interviews. The type of problem that works well should be linked to regular tasks that IT hires will be doing; this can be writing code, solving bugs, breaking through code issues, redefining software or hardware, and so on.

Understand your solution and the skills needed to resolve the problem

You obviously want to not only have a complex problem, but also the solution to the problem, so you can work out which participant has done well, having an expectation around the time frame and level of skills needed. Once you have decided on your problem, you will automatically know the kind of participant skills needed to resolve your challenge. If you set a coding problem, by default you are looking for people with coding skills in a particular language. If it is a systems design or engineering challenge, the skills you are looking for are system-design-related.

Communicate your competition

So, the next step is to communicate your event with your target audience. If you have set up social media, by all means, communicate it through that medium; providing you have enough followers, you will find some participants via these channels. With most companies you may need to go further than this, by reaching out to local universities and colleges. You could host preliminaries in these institutions, with a final showdown of winners from across your channels, or just host the event in one location and invite all participants.

Competition logistics

Typically, because you are talking about an IT-related problem, you will need enough equipment for each participant, which may mean availability of computers with the problem installed. Thus, having a college venue may be ideal, or alternatively your premises, if you have a spacious meeting room. Going to external hotels or conference centers may require a lot more preparation; so if you are new to competition hosting, keep the numbers low and manageable.

Competition judges and prize

The final elements for a successful competition are judges and a prize. The judges may have different things to look out for, but at least one judge needs to know the technological solutions and the level of skill it takes to resolve something, to add to this weighting. You may have others looking at your problem-solving ability, attitude, and approach. At the end of the day, a competition means that you choose a winner, so you want to know the criteria you look for in the selection process, which can be as simple as the first candidate who fixes the problem. The prize can be winning an internship or a contract with your organization for a particular role.

While the first employees at Facebook were hired through a competition, these days their competitions rarely lead to interviews. I would recommend that you consider this for internships and trainee programs, so you still have time to judge the regular performance of a candidate. Hiring straight from a competition may not give you enough insight into a candidate's full profile. However, your competition will create a buzz and awareness of your company, which may have gone unnoticed before, so ensure that your invitations stand out and reach as many of your target group as possible, and also show creativity.

These days IT companies use hack-fests or developer days to work on innovations; what you could do is ask university students to take part alongside existing employees of your firm. Once again, you will create a view of your company that stands out from the norm, and the students will gain an insight into real-life problem solving by collaborating with employees. Your employees, on the other hand, may come away with new ideas and potential recommendations for new hires.

Tip

Create a buzz about your event with video clips of the CEO or hiring manager explaining what you are looking for in candidates distributed through social media.

Sell the opportunity to outshine your peers with the ultimate prize of a job opportunity for the winner.

Games

As an extension to organizing a skills-based competition, some companies have resorted to creating a full-blown computer or video game to test their future employees. This approach will require a budget to outsource actual game creation to a games studio, unless of course you have in-house game developers. The same rules apply as mentioned previously; you need to be very clear on the purpose of the game and what skills you are testing.

The design of a game starts typically with a games concept brief, which contains the following elements:

> **High concept**: A short description of the purpose of the game

> **Features**: Bullet points that describe the player's experience or gameplay

> **Player motivation**: This identifies what the player's goals and objectives are in the game

> **Design goals**: This is how the game will look and feel to the player

> **Target hardware**: What platform the game will work on, with computer or video as the most common platforms for businesses

The reason to resort to a game in the recruitment process can be to simulate behaviors that are life-like through a game, which Marriott did with their Facebook-based game called "My Marriott Hotel". The game effectively allows players to run their own virtual hotel, hire and fire staff, deliver food, and look after rooms. The happier the guests, the higher the score.

Make a note

If you would like to test your skills in hotel management, you need to have a Facebook account and after that just follow this link:

`https://apps.facebook.com/mymarriotthotel/`.

Or, you can simply look for the My Marriott Hotel app on Facebook.

Marriott struggled to attract employees in international markets and researched how they could best connect with their target audience of 17 to 24 year olds willing to work in a hotel environment. Their social game has become very successful and has assisted the organization to attract the kind of talent they were looking for.

Another example where a game was used effectively for recruitment is the French postal service **Formaposte**. They experienced a high dropout rate of new hires—nearly a quarter of new hires stopped working after the initial trial period. With the game called Jeu Facteur Academy, they let potential hires experience a week in the life of their new postal career from getting up early to come in to work, nudging players to make the right choices along the way, and how to interact with customers and managers. Essentially, they managed the expectations of new hires and as a result brought their dropout rate down from 25 percent to 8 percent.

Make a note

If you speak French, you can be a postman for a week on this link:

`www.formaposte-iledefrance.fr/jeu-facteur-academy./`

When embarking on this route, you will need to be prepared to go through a number of reviews and test phases to make sure all your requirements are working well and the game delivers on its promise.

Sponsoring student projects

Each year, students will have to create a number of group activities, and for many courses, a final year project is required. Typically, students decide in year three or the beginning of year four, of a four-year degree program, what their final year project will be. For a company, you have an opportunity here to create an early liaison and potentially spot a future employee.

The steps involved in pursuing this kind of action are as follows:

1. Approach your local university and third-level institutions.
2. Find out the requirements of projects as part of the course curriculum.
3. Connect with lecturers.
4. Find out if projects from a local organization would be welcomed.
5. Find out the project requirements.

In my experience, most of the time this will be highly encouraged, as long as it can somehow fit or link in with the course material.

One option would be to give the whole class the same project and look for multiple outcomes, which may result in additional time being spent on evaluation, and possibly a lot of repetition. Alternatively, you may ask for the best students to work on your project or use a competition to select a winning team.

The key to making it worthwhile for both you and the students is to give them a real-life scenario and invite them to your organization, so they can find out first-hand what the challenges and constraints are, or ask existing employees questions. If you are looking for completely independent feedback, the key is to provide them with enough information to start off with and specifications as to what format you want them to use when sending you back results, with the added expectation of innovation.

The more you interact with the student group, the likelier you are to spot a potential employee. The added bonus of being involved with students at this stage is the interest you'll generate in relation to your organization, and the type of work you do, which may result in spontaneous applications when graduation comes around.

Meeting students in their environment

In order to gain interest from students, they first of all need to know that you exist. Depending on the size of your organization, they may not realize you exist or, if they know about your company, they may not know that you have IT positions available. So, one of the most tried, tested, and long-standing approaches is to give career talks at local universities, provide information to career guidance officers with application forms, and if the university holds what is also known as a "milk round", where companies can come and meet with the top graduates before graduation, you should be a part of these options.

You can find the relevant information through the career guidance office, which most reputable institutes will have. In the case that a dedicated officer is not available, connect with the head of the department of the relevant courses and offer career talks or company insight presentations.

What large IT organizations are doing is targeting specific universities with a roadshow. If you look at the Microsoft career pages, they visit universities with a number of events from general information to educational, and some just pure fun-oriented. So, have a think about what you can achieve in your current time resources, budget, and reach.

If budget and time are an issue, I recommend you just stick to giving presentations to specific groups of students that are in your target application audience. If you can afford something more, such as sponsoring an IT society event, or organizing an original event on campus, for example, a hack fest or a fun-oriented event, may well be an option.

Tip
For students to apply, they need to know you, like you, and understand that you may have a job going that is of interest to them.

Summary

In this chapter, we have learned how to:

➤ Create an attractive online presence

➤ Host a successful apprenticeship, internship, or trainee program

➤ Organize a competition or hack-fest

➤ Sponsor a student project

➤ Meet students in their environments

In the next chapter, we bring the whole process together with best practice techniques on running an effective recruitment process and turning a candidate into an employee.

4

Getting to "You're Hired"

The recruitment process isn't vastly different from the dating process; you want your company to look attractive to the opposite side, which is what we spoke about in *Chapter 2, Be Clear on What Your Organization Has to Offer*. Then, you want to provide opportunities for them to meet with you and get to know you better, which was dealt with in *Chapter 3, Creativity Rules in Gaining Graduate Interest*. So, in this chapter, we want to take the next step from the first date to, hopefully, a long-term relationship.

You will learn about timing in the recruitment process, screening candidates, and interview practices. Once you have narrowed down your choices, I will share the next steps with you to make sure you eliminate risks and surprises on the path to hiring the right candidate for your company and the job.

I would expect that by engaging in some of the steps of the previous chapters, you will have attracted the interest of IT graduates, and they will have chosen to apply for a position at your firm, either through your online application process or with their CV and hopefully a cover letter.

Time is of the essence

Time is of the essence once you have had a job opportunity advertised for a few weeks, especially because you are attracting the connected generation, who will lose interest when responsiveness is lacking. I suggest you include a closing date for applications, but start the selection process as you start receiving applications. The first ones to respond tend to be actively looking and may have had your company on their shortlist of preferred employers. Thanks to the functionality of social media, some search engines allow job seekers to set preferences and follow companies.

If you can thank candidates for their application as soon as it comes in, and respond with a time frame within which you will be processing them this sends a bit of positive news to the candidates. It also lets them know that you received their application and the date by which they can expect to be called for an interview. You can even indicate by when they can assume that they have not been shortlisted for this process. I prefer to tell people in a personal and respectful note that they weren't successful, but I see a lot of companies also using a standard e-mail response, or including in their initial receipt of application message that if the candidate hasn't heard back from them by x date, the application was not successful this time. It depends entirely on the volume of applications you receive and also the perception you want to give of your organization in the marketplace. If one of your values is concentrated on treating your customer well and responding on time, then this is an area where you should invest a bit of effort.

The timing between the first contact and the actual offer, for graduate recruitment, should be somewhere between a few weeks and up to a maximum of two months. The longer the process, the more likely your candidate will look elsewhere and thus lose interest in your company. Slow decision-making in this process may also indicate an underlying level of bureaucracy or indecisiveness, which the current generation of applicants isn't very patient about.

Quite a few IT students will start applying for jobs in their final year, so they have an offer waiting for them as soon as they complete their exams, particularly the best and more ambitious students. So, advertise your positions early in the calendar year (January to March), with a view to having a fresh graduate start straight after their exams or after a summer break.

Narrowing down your selection

Let's hope that your previous activities have created a bit of interest in your organization and that when your job posting opens, you receive a number of applicants. If you hit the success level of the likes of Google, you may receive hundreds of applications for any one position, so narrowing down the selection will be essential.

If you have followed some of the advice given in *Chapter 2, Be Clear on What Your Organization Has to Offer*, you will have a good idea of the kind of person you are looking for, as well as their skills and attributes. So, the first step is to compare the applications against your own criteria. You may notice some great fits and potentially some wild cards, as well as some that just don't fit what you are after. You need to involve the direct manager for the new role in order to create the shortlist together.

Creating a shortlist

Selection software does exist, which matches CVs and application forms against key words based on your job description. The only drawback I see is that you will not spot a potential wild card, but if the volume of applications is a challenge, then this may be a minimal challenge.

Telephone screening

Once you have created a shortlist, the current practice is then to do a phone screening, where some additional details are double-checked, such as their motivation to apply, potential start date, salary expectations, other companies that they have applied to, a quick review of their CV, and a questioning of any obvious gaps in their CV. The applicants that fit, both in terms of enthusiasm and start dates that you have on offer, then go through to the next round. If you are recruiting graduates for their first job, not all of them will come with experience, but their extra-curricular activities and hobbies may provide enough information to establish a picture about the individual.

Tip
Treat your applicants with dignity and respect thank them for applying, even when they aren't successful, and let them know where they stand.

The first date

Once you have shortlisted the candidates, you want to invite them for a first real interview. With current technology this can take place over Skype, or on Google Hangout, or Face Time, or the traditional in-person way. Failure to use modern technology will give a bad impression to this generation, so make sure you test the technology first. Failure may well indicate to a Millennial that the company is not as up-to-date as they would like them to be. Depending on the number of applicants on the shortlist, you can choose any of these options.

As a guideline, online interviews are a good medium when both parties have a good Internet connection, so if this is poor then in-person may be your best option. Online interviews tend to be shorter than in-person interviews because the candidates and the interviewers tend to come straight to the point, whereas face-to-face situations are more polite and interviewers are expected to engage in settling visible nerves through small talk.

Competency-based interviews

The most often used interview technique is behavioral or competency-based questioning. What you are basically trying to find out from a candidate is how they would behave in a particular situation, or how they have dealt with a scenario in the past. The following are some examples of this:

> ➤ Explain a situation where you had to finish work under pressure
> ➤ Imagine the scenario where you have a problem you never encountered before; how would you start dealing with this?
> ➤ Tell me about a time where you clearly demonstrated your ability to be innovative

The whole idea is that you get the candidate talking through their CV and life, with practical examples of skills and attributes that you are actively looking for. Personally, I have experienced this kind of interview only in the last five years, which also means that most students should be prepared to go through them. I would be open about the way you interview. Again, this tends to be standard practice in the IT industry; both Google and Microsoft have a page in their career section that explains how their recruitment process works. Google even includes YouTube clips about the process, so if you are looking for further inspiration, I suggest you start there.

Repeat the interview process with a number of employees from your company and in each round, look to narrow down your selection.

The skills test

It is normal for a technical area, especially when you are expecting a candidate to come with a particular kind of skill, to test their ability in this area. In some organizations, this skills test is put before the first interview, in order to save time during the process. However, there is no rule when you do it, but I would just recommend that you do it. For example, hold a coding test to verify that they know the basics of writing a simple program, similar to what you would expect them to do in a real job.

If you have used a coding challenge, hack-fest, or game to test skills, you already have an insight into your candidate; we described all these options in *Chapter 3, Creativity Rules in Gaining Graduate Interest*. The types of skills to test are job-related skills, and at a graduate level, such as engineering challenges, software application tests, and problem-solving skills relevant to the role. You can include interpersonal skills such as collaboration, influencing, and giving presentations, especially when they are key to performing well on the job.

The Millennial generation has grown up with various kinds of games and has probably spent as much time playing those as educating themselves to the level they are at. What games have taught them is instant and regular feedback, collaboration if they are a multiplayer gamer, and problem-solving abilities. Hence, applicants will expect and look for feedback on their performance, and the best way to deal with this is to be willing to give them constructive feedback on their test performance.

Make a note

In a nutshell:

Test essential skills for the job

Set the test level at a reasonably expected level for a graduate

Give feedback after the test

Getting to "You're hired!"

Once you have completed an initial screening, behavioral style interviews, and skills testing, you should have a shortlist in single figures or ideally, even a clear favorite that you want to hire.

Conducting a reference check

I would recommend that the next step would be a reference check, especially if the candidates have been employed before. You could also get a character reference from a sports coach or teacher to get a day-to-day insight into the person. The purpose of a reference check is to look for confirmation of the skills and attitude that you have witnessed in the interview process. Most people will give you a positive reflection, but when it is decidedly neutral or negative, you may want to investigate your candidate somewhat further.

Making an offer

Once you are satisfied that you have found a candidate who is a good fit for your company, the team, and has the appropriate level of skills to be hired, you need to make them an offer.

Job offers these days tend to be made first verbally over the phone, and when you receive a positive answer from the candidate, then a formal letter with a contract enclosed is sent either in the post or by e-mail. You request that the candidate send back a signed copy and to confirm that the start date you have in mind is indeed suitable for them.

Negotiating the salary and package

Salary and package negotiations are expected to have been covered earlier on in the recruitment process; stating the salary and benefit package up front in the first screening interview will outline whether you expect negotiations or not. Some students may, once they see the details in writing, try to increase or change some of the package. Use your discretion and judgment to see if this is an option. To give my own example, I write for fun (blogs, books, articles, and so on), but also for payment, so any employer offering me a role will need to be made aware that I do this on the side and I usually look for a written approval of this, so I don't have any surprises later in the game. Because freedom and independence is important to this generation, be aware that they may have more than one interest at the same time, and it may be the differentiator between the acceptance and rejection of your offer.

The candidate accepted, now what?

The candidate has accepted your offer, you have a start date, and you now need to make sure that you are ready to welcome them. I consider the first few weeks on a new job still part of the evaluation process on both sides. So give your company and the candidate the best chance of success by putting some thoughts into their induction period. Remember that this is the connected online generation, so where possible invite them into social media internal groups and stay connected with them.

Welcome the new hire

Once your offer has been accepted and the contract has been returned, you need to set the wheels in motion to welcome a new hire on their first day. If their start date is a few months away, my advice is to start including them in company events, newsletters, and generally keep in touch. A nice touch is a good luck card before their exams and a well done after the exams, once you know they have passed.

The following are some of my suggestions for a welcome start:

➤ Who will welcome the new hire? Inform them and the new hire

➤ Arrange meet and greet opportunities for the new hire, with team members and other employees they may work with closely

➤ Introduce them to how the business works, from the viewpoint of different departments

➤ Ensure they have their equipment (computer, phone, security access, and so on)

➤ Ensure they have access to software, shared drives, and so on, so they can be productive

➤ Team them up with a mentor, who can teach them what is expected

➤ Invite them for lunch on the first few days, so they get to know more people

Summary

In this chapter we took you from the application all the way through to the first few days on the job for your new recruit.

The key topics you learned in this chapter were:

➤ The importance of timing as part of the recruitment process

➤ Narrowing down your shortlist

➤ Competency-based interviews

➤ Skills testing

➤ Final steps of making an offer

➤ Welcoming your candidate

What should be clear at this stage is that the future generation of workers is Internet-savvy, always connected, and looking for more than just a role that pays the bills. They want the organization to fit their values and life as much as the other way around. Attracting IT graduates and at that, attracting the best, will be an exercise in creativity and communication.

I hope that this book has given you some useful ideas on how to start and smooth out your process to lead to long-lasting employee relationships, and to successfully attract more IT graduates to join your company.

www.ingramcontent.com/pod-product-compliance
Lightning Source LLC
LaVergne TN
LVHW081349050326
832903LV00024B/1376